Dig and Tip

Pauline Cartwright

Look at this.
It can dig.

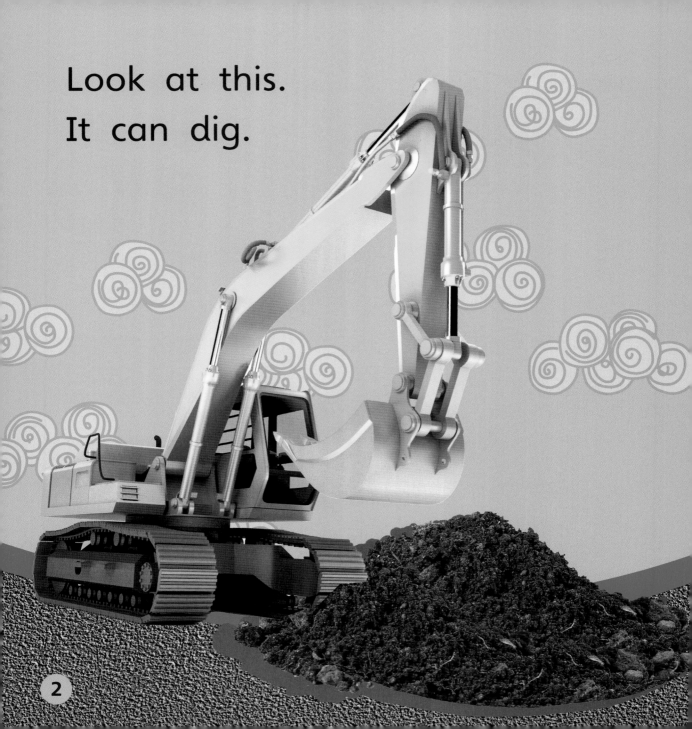

Look at this.
It can tip.

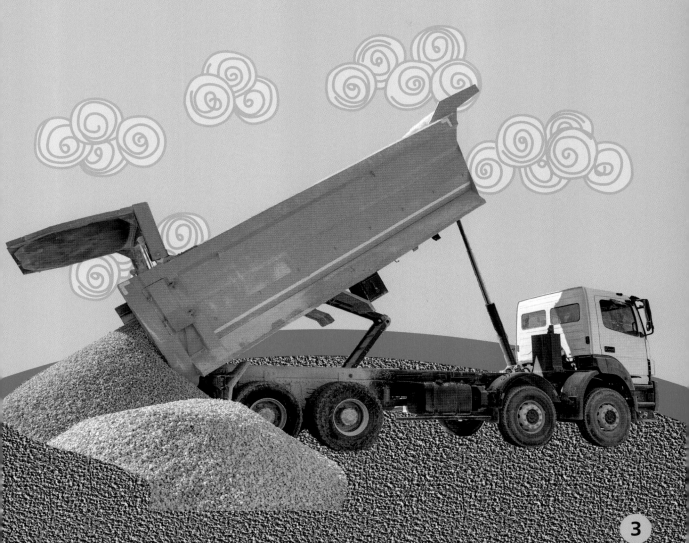

Look at this.
It can push.

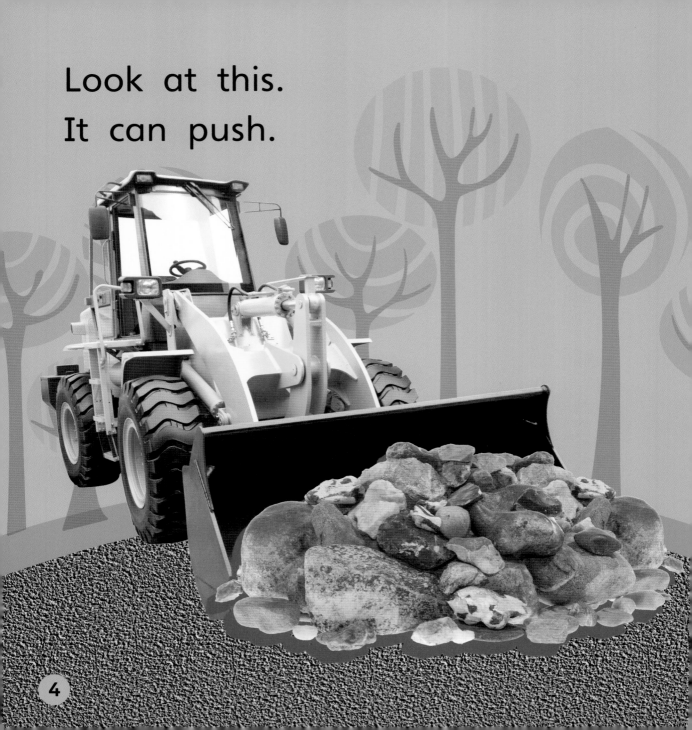

Look at this.
It can roll.

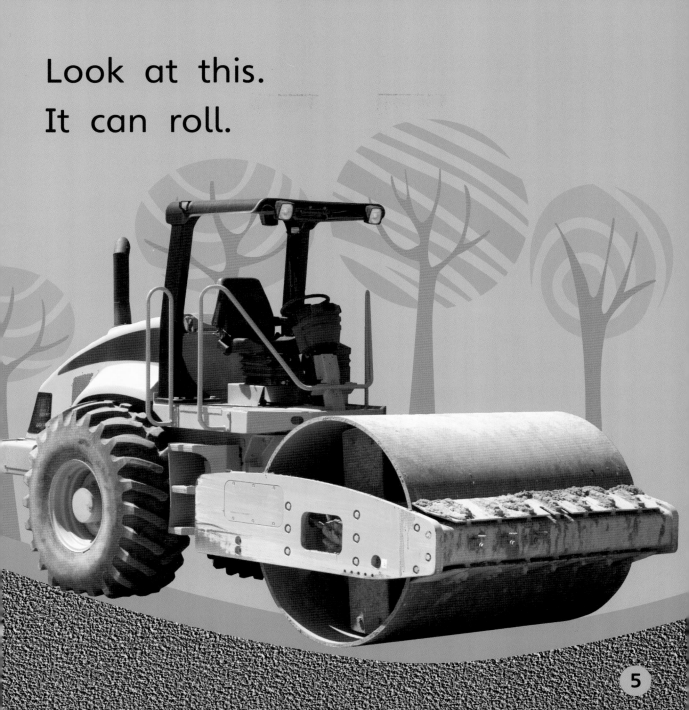

Look at this.
It can tip, too.

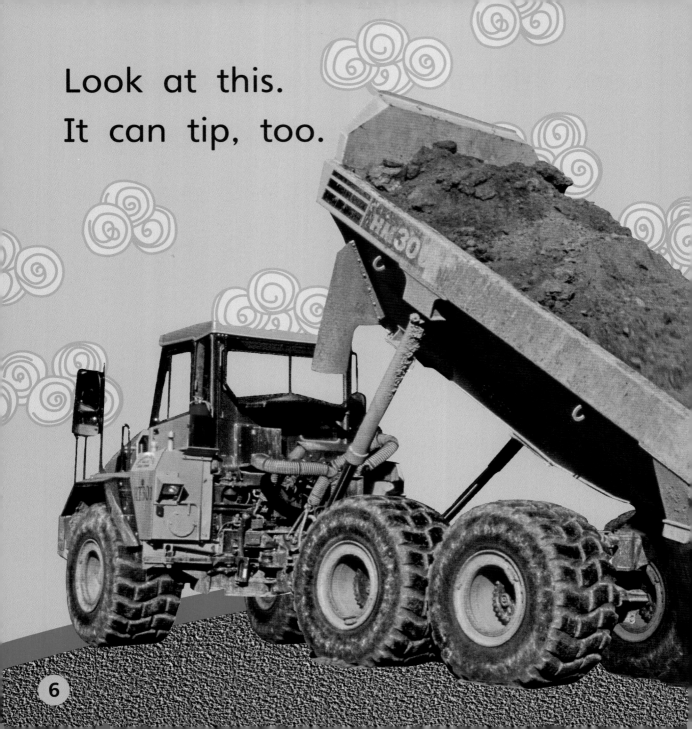

Look at this.
It can go.

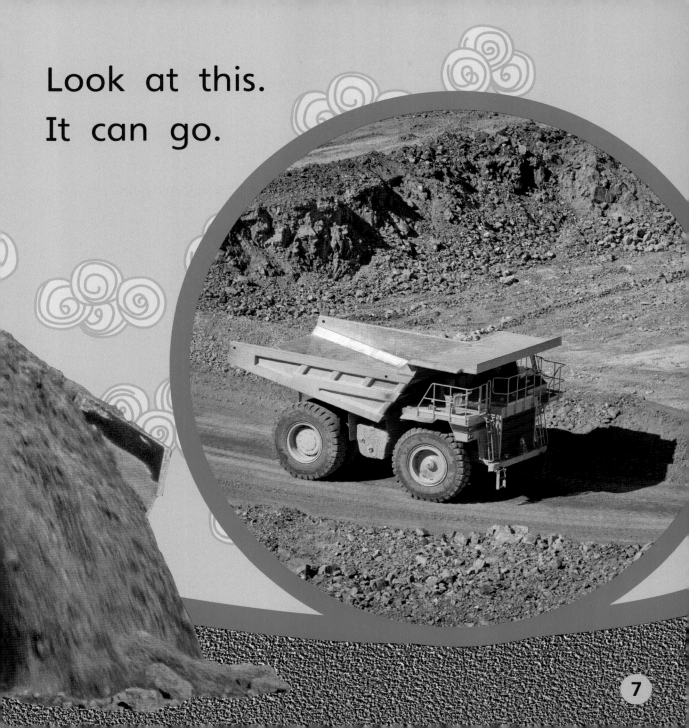

dig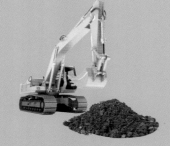

push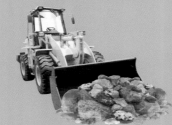

roll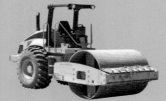

tip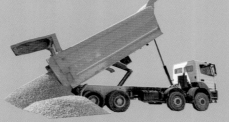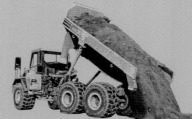